6/14

W9-BWI-230

BLAZERS

THE WORLD OF ROBOTS

# ROBOTS IN RISKY JOBS

## ON THE BATTLEFIELD AND BEYOND

BY KATHRYN CLAY

Consultant:
Barbara J. Fox
Professor Emerita
North Carolina State University

CAPSTONE PRESS
a capstone imprint

Blazers Books are published by Capstone Press,
1710 Roe Crest Drive, North Mankato, Minnesota 56003
www.capstonepub.com

**Library of Congress Cataloging-in-Publication Data**
Clay, Kathryn.
Robots in risky jobs : on the battlefield and beyond / by Kathryn Clay.
pages cm.—(Blazers books. The world of robots)
Includes bibliographical references and index.
Summary: "Describes various military, space, and other robots used to carry out
missions that are too dangerous for human beings"—Provided by publisher
Audience: Grades 4–6.
ISBN 978-1-4765-3972-0 (library binding)
ISBN 978-1-4765-51123-8 (paperback)
ISBN 978-1-4765-5953-7 (ebook PDF)
1. Robots—Juvenile literature. 2. Military robots—Juvenile literature. I. Title
TJ211.2.C55 2013
629.8′92—dc23                                                      2013026493

**Editorial Credits**
Aaron Sautter, editor; Ted Williams, designer; Eric Gohl, media researcher;
Eric Manske, production specialist

**Photo Credits**
Courtesy of Boston Dynamics: 17, 28; DVIC: USAF/TSGT Effrain Lopez, 21,
USAF/TSGT Michele A. Desrochers, cover (bottom right), US Navy/MC2 Gary
Granger Jr., 15; Getty Images: AFP/Toshifumi Kitamura, 8; NASA: cover (bottom
left), 23, JPL/Cornell University, 27, JPL-Caltech, 25, JPL-Caltech/Malin Space
Science Systems, 26; Newscom: Getty Images/AFP/NASA, 7, Getty Images/AFP/
STR, 4, ZOB WENN Photos/CB2, 19; NOAA: AUVfest 2008/Partnership Runs
Deep, Navy, 13; Science Source: Peter Menzel, 11; Shutterstock: Ivan Nikulin,
cover (top)

Printed in the United States of America in Stevens Point, Wisconsin.
092013        007768WZS14

# TABLE OF
# CONTENTS

The Japanese T-53 Enryu robot is useful for lifting and moving heavy objects.

# ROBOTS TO THE RESCUE!

What do you do in a risky situation to rescue people in danger? Send in the **robots**! Each day robots are used for many dangerous jobs.

**robot**—a machine programmed to do jobs usually performed by a person

# ROBOT RESCUERS

## URBIE

Some robots help search disaster areas. Urbie is a small search-and-rescue robot. Urbie can crawl through small spaces in wrecked buildings. It uses built-in cameras to search for survivors.

## ROBOT FACT
Some rescue robots look and move like snakes. They slide under doors and through tiny spaces.

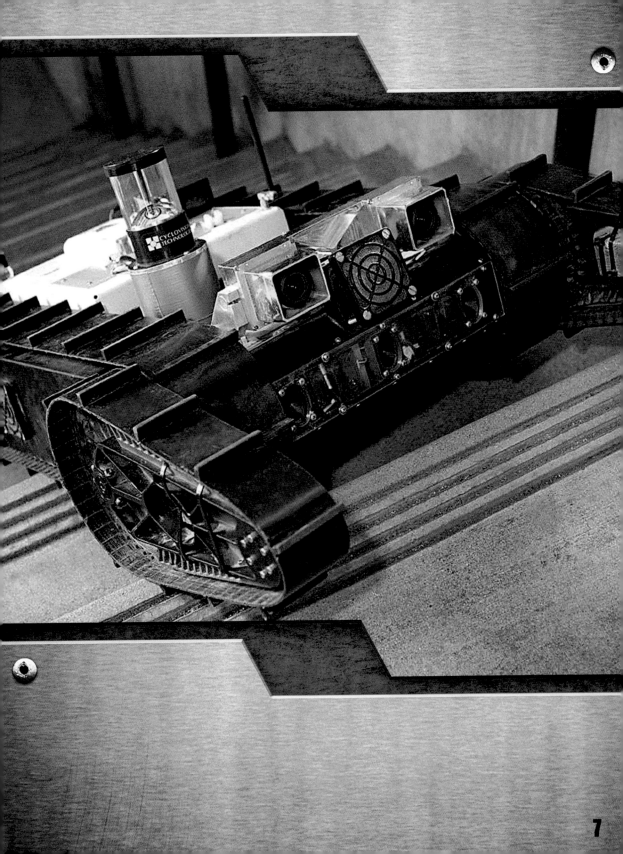

ROBOT FACT

Enryu means "rescue dragon" in Japanese.

北九州市消防局

8

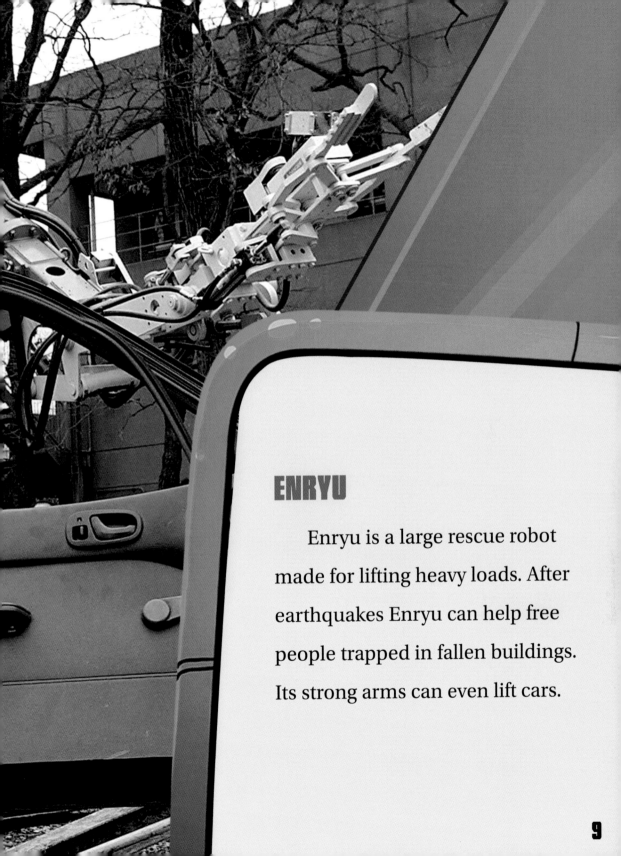

## ENRYU

Enryu is a large rescue robot made for lifting heavy loads. After earthquakes Enryu can help free people trapped in fallen buildings. Its strong arms can even lift cars.

# Exploring the Ocean

## REMOTELY OPERATED VEHICLES (ROVs)

ROVs dive to the deepest parts of the ocean. Operators use **remote controls** and cameras to steer the robots. Some ROVs are used to explore the ocean floor or search sunken ships.

**remote control**—a device used to control machines from a distance

# ROBOT FACT

Ariel is a six-legged robot that moves forward, backward, and sideways just like a crab. It is being designed to find and explode mines in the water near shorelines.

# AUTONOMOUS UNDERWATER VEHICLES (AUVs)

No human operators? No problem. **Autonomous** Underwater Vehicles (AUVs) control themselves. They measure water depths, ocean **currents**, and water temperatures.

**autonomous**—able to control oneself; autonomous robots are not operated by remote control

**current**—the movement of water in a river or an ocean

# ROBOTS ON THE BATTLEFIELD

## TALON

Military robots help keep soldiers safe on the battlefield. Small TALON robots carry **infrared cameras** to search for enemy fighters inside buildings. TALONs also help soldiers disarm bombs from a distance.

**infrared camera**—a camera that locates objects by heat

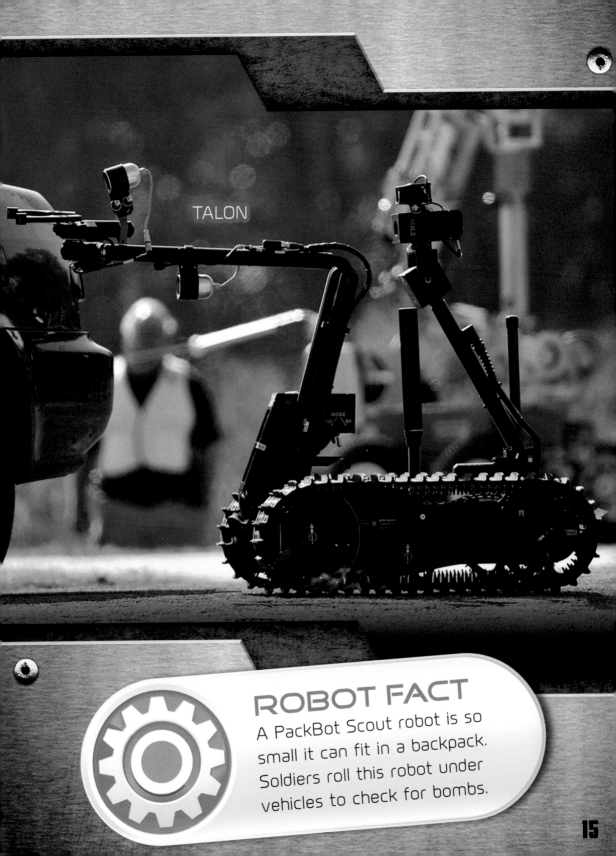

TALON

## ROBOT FACT

A PackBot Scout robot is so small it can fit in a backpack. Soldiers roll this robot under vehicles to check for bombs.

## ALPHADOG

AlphaDog carries supplies over long distances. It looks like a large dog without a head. The four-legged robot can walk across sand, snow, mud, and ice.

# BEAR

The Battlefield Extraction-Assist Robot (BEAR) carries wounded soldiers to safety. BEAR can lift about 500 pounds (227 kg). Soldiers also use BEAR to carry supplies and hunt for **booby traps**.

**booby trap**—a hidden trap or explosive device that is triggered when someone or something touches it

# UNMANNED AERIAL VEHICLES (UAVs)

Soldiers operate UAVs by remote control. UAVs carry cameras to help find and spy on enemies. Some UAVs also carry weapons to attack targets from the air.

MQ-1 Predator UAV

DCC: SRA M. MUNGUIA
ADCC: SRA C. BOWMAN

## ROBOT FACT

Military UAVs carry cameras that can read a license plate up to 2 miles (3.2 km) away.

# SPACE EXPLORERS

## CANADARM 2

Robots often help scientists study and explore space. The Canadarm 2 is a large robotic arm attached to the *International Space Station (ISS).* Astronauts use it to move large objects and help maintain the station.

## ROBOT FACT

The *International Space Station* was built by several countries. Astronauts live and work there to learn more about space.

# ORBITERS AND LANDERS

The *Cassini* **orbiter** reached Saturn in 2004. It sent the *Huygens* **lander** to Titan, Saturn's largest moon. The lander found liquid **methane** lakes on the moon.

**orbiter**—a spacecraft that orbits a planet or other space objects

**lander**—a spacecraft that lands on an object to study the surface

**methane**—colorless, flammable gas; methane becomes a liquid at extremely cold temperatures

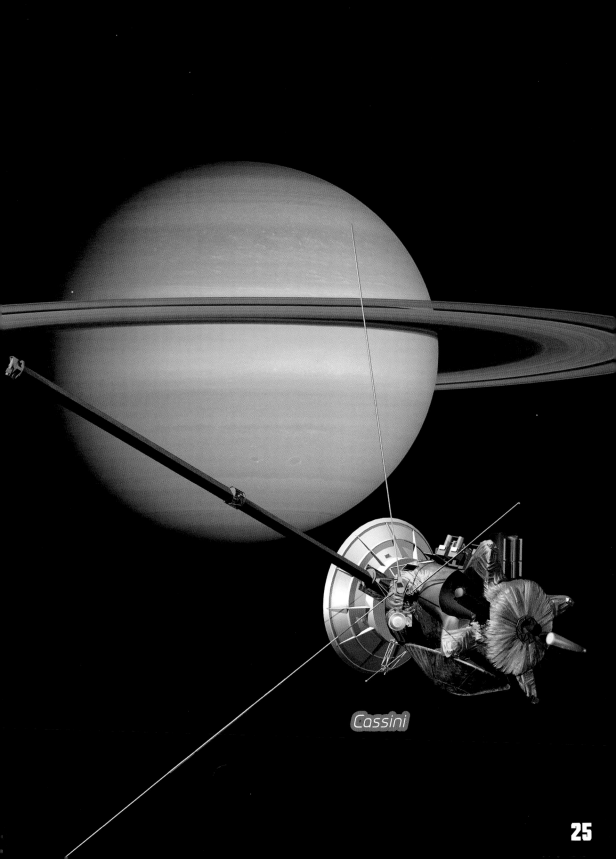

Cassini

# ROVERS

The *Curiosity* rover landed on Mars in August 2012. Earlier Mars rovers were small. But *Curiosity* is the size of a car. The rover uses a **laser** to study rocks and soil.

Curiosity

*Opportunity*

## ROBOT FACT

The *Spirit* and *Opportunity* rovers landed on Mars in 2004. *Spirit* explored Mars' surface until 2010. *Opportunity* still studies the planet today.

**laser**—a thin, intense, high-energy beam of light

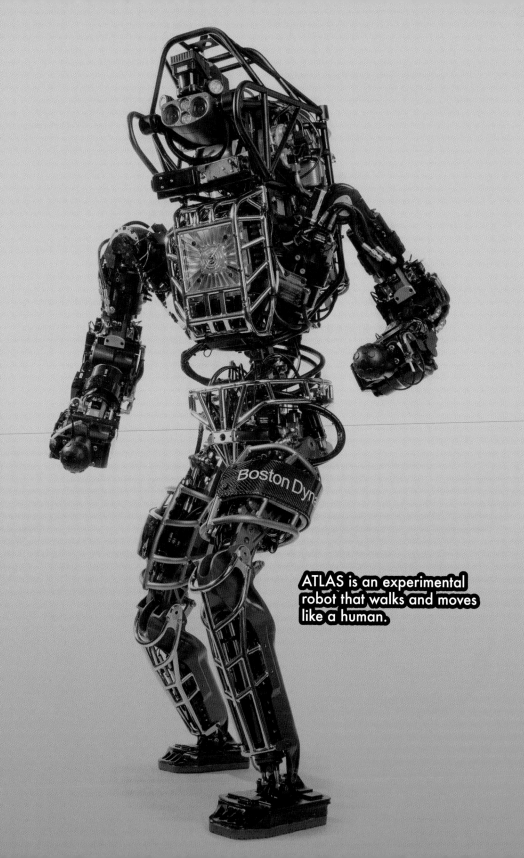

ATLAS is an experimental robot that walks and moves like a human.

## FUTURE ROBOT RISK TAKERS

Some robots may move and act more like people in the future. They may even think for themselves. But no matter how they are designed, robots will keep doing dangerous jobs to keep people safe.

## ROBOT FACT
The U.S. military is working on small insectlike robots to spy on enemies.

# GLOSSARY

**autonomous** (aw-TAH-nuh-muhss)—able to control oneself; autonomous robots are not operated by remote control

**booby trap** (BOO-bee TRAP)—a hidden trap or explosive device that is triggered when someone or something touches it

**current** (KUHR-uhnt)—the movement of water in a river or an ocean

**infrared camera** (in-fruh-RED KAM-ur-uh)—a camera that locates objects by heat

**lander** (LAND-uhr)—a spacecraft that lands on an object to study the surface

**laser** (LAY-zur)—a thin, intense, high-energy beam of light

**methane** (meth-AYN)—colorless, flammable gas; methane becomes a liquid at extremely cold temperatures

**mine** (MINE)—an explosive device; land mines are buried underground; water mines float in the water

**orbiter** (OR-bit-ur)—a spacecraft that orbits a planet or other space objects

**remote control** (ri-MOHT kuhn-TROHL)—a device used to control machines from a distance

**robot** (ROH-bot)—a machine programmed to do jobs usually performed by a person

# READ MORE

**Alpert, Barbara.** *U.S. Military Robots.* U.S. Military Technology. Mankato, Minn.: Capstone Press, 2013.

**Kortenkamp, Steve.** *Space Robots.* Incredible Space. Mankato, Minn.: Capstone Press, 2009.

**Parker, Steve.** *Robots in Space.* RobotWorld. Mankato, Minn.: Amicus, 2011.

# INTERNET SITES

FactHound offers a safe, fun way to find Internet sites related to this book. All of the sites on FactHound have been researched by our staff.

Here's all you do:

Visit *www.facthound.com*

Type in this code: 9781476539720

Check out projects, games and lots more at
**www.capstonekids.com**

# INDEX